How to Build an Extraordinary Relationship with Your Partner

A Step By Step Relationship Guide to Building a Strong Bond with Your Partner

Mitchell Browne

TABLE OF CONTENTS

Dedication

To every single out there, hoping on having a beautiful and extraordinary successful lasting relationship with their next partner.

May you have all of that and something even more great than you have dreamt.

To those in a relationship, hoping to find the love ignite again. It surely will. Do not give up on working on your relationship.

Acknowledgement

Many thanks to my husband, Matthew, through whom I have learn a lot of things that has to do with building up a strong relationship. You are a great and patient teacher. I love you.

To Becca, my editor who painstakingly edit this book. You are awesome.

To Sam, my friend who despite been very busy always makes out time to read my book. I cherish you a lot.

To all my readers, I love you all. I write for you.

Introduction

Every one of us craves an extraordinary relationship. Something magical, almost nonexistent of this world. Perhaps something from a fairy tale land or Harlequin books. We want to have a relationship that is nurture and fulfilled with love.

But few of us understand how to find and keep that love and relationship. Perhaps we understand the act of falling in love, which to me is the easiest but how to keep in love?

To remain in love?

We all want results, but do not know the practical steps to take to get there.

Truth is if you want to create an extraordinary relationship with your partner, the effort start with you. Yes, you.

You must start with yourself. Remember a relationship isn't a place you go to get something, it is a place you go to… to give. But many are ignorant of this.

You go into a relationship to give your undivided attention, to give your love, your energy and your heart.

After all, isn't it one of the beauty of nature that when you give so much, you get even more in return.

You then create passion, joy, trust and an intimacy that surpass every obstacle and every challenge that may come your way. And even in your darkest moments, your relationship's journey become a blessing and a gift that allows you and your partner to become stronger as an entity.

Do you want to truly becomes a better partner in a relationship and enjoy an extraordinary relationship with your partner? Then there are few fundamental steps to follow, which has been summed up in this book.

Preface

The hashtag #RelationshipGoals has become a more common trend than it was many years ago. It is now a topic trending worldwide. The evidence of this is on social media where one doesn't need to type the complete words, before the search engine pop up with lots of suggestion on relationship goals, displaying pictures of lovers cuddled up romantically, sharing cute kisses, holding hands in park, stargazing, having dinner in a five star restaurant with all elegance and sign of love in the air. All cutes pictures depicting a relationship that has never been anything but rosy and pure bliss.

Then what comes to mind? Oh I want this kind of a relationship. The most common trend this day is when people came across such beautiful relationship pictures was asking "God when" literally meaning, when can they have a love and relationship just like the one they have seen on the medias, watched in a movie, read in a mills and boons novel or even seen around them.

I bet we all want a relationship like this, a sweet relationship like that of Will and Jada, Kim and Kanye, Prince Harry and Megan. I mean we all have that imagination of the kind of sweet love relationship that we want., perhaps a tall handsomely built man who takes you on a shopping spree and pays the bill every time or a beautiful lady with hazel eyes that turns the head like Nicki or Rihana is the imagination of a lover you have painted.

Now don't look defensive and ask me what is wrong with such imagination. No, it's totally okay to want all of that, we all want to have that ideal relationship and take those perfect pictures, post it with the hashtag #relationshipgoals but let me ask you.

What if all that you see was just an illusion?

What if all this perfect appearing relationship are just mirage?

What if those relationship are built on unstable bond that are bound to fall eventually?

To hit the nail, what if all that you see around and yearn for was just a camouflage? An illusion the society sells to portray a perfect intimate relationship

But what if I tell you that a there are steps to help you achieve that perfect relationship. A steps that reveals why and how a human connection is important and how to achieve it.

This is why you need to read this book.

Determination

Why Determination?

Often time you could have heard the saying that the most powerful driving force to a successful life or achieving almost an impossible goals is your strong will, in other words, your determination which is also your courage. This is the most important of all the virtues because without courage, you can't practice any other virtue consistently.

What is determination?

Determination is a positive emotional feeling that involves persevering towards a difficult goal in spite of obstacles. Determination occurs prior to goal attainment and serves to motivate behavior that will help achieve one's goal.

A determined mind is one that has won half the journey even before it embark on it. This determination to win is often the better part of winning. Your determination to succeed at having a good relationship is as good and necessary as the steps you are going to take towards having that good relationship.

After all, there is this quote that says if we attack our problems with determination, we shall succeed.

Building a good relationship needs determination, the determination to succeed at it despite all odd. No relationship is a bed of roses. The celebrity who goes all and about talking and posting great pictures on relationship goals won't tell you about the ugly side of that relationship. You must know that nothing is ever easy without already having it difficult.

If you see people enjoying the kind of relationship you crave for, did you stop and ask yourself what it took them to come thus far? The sacrifices they made. Then would you be willing to make the same?

If you haven't already think thus far. I pose it to you now, how determined are you to make your relationship extraordinary?

How determined are you to sacrifice for having a great relationship?

If you answer "Very determined" to the above question, then congratulations to you because you already half way towards having that successful relationship. I mean you already took half the steps and the remaining half is in putting everything you will learn in this book to practice.

Before You Meet That Person

Pardon me, but I will be asking a lot of questions in the process of our journey together.

You want an extraordinary relationship, do you not? Then let me ask you. How ready are you?

No, do not just tell me you are ready because you are of the age. What age? Relationship having age or marriageable age?

Maybe on that, you have meet up, but on all other aspects which are more important and essential, how ready and prepared are you?

Mentally, are you?

Financially, are you?

Emotionally, are you?

These are questions you need to ask yourself before you take that step. You cannot succeed at something you haven't prepared yourself for.

Oh, maybe some people do, but that is one in a million chance. Not a chance you should be willing to take.

Before you find or meet that perfect someone, you have to be prepared for him or her. So many people enter into relationships without a defined goals, without preparedness, and at the end discovered that they are dating the wrong person.

This often happens because we make some fundamental mistakes when we are single and seeking a romantic relationship, in most cases, it is the rush to feel all the feelings, to experience all the lovey dovey moments that leads to these mistakes.

The perfect relationship should begin long before you met that special someone. It is only when you are ready and prepared in all aspect and have your relationships goals and aspiration well defined that you can now be sure to move towards finding that perfect person for you.

Preparing yourself for true love starts with changing your perspective about what true love really is and by healing yourself in order to show up in the world in equal vibration to what you'd like to attract.

Preparing for a relationship is just as important as preparing for anything else in your life. You have to be ready for it if it's going to actually work out. Imagine going for a job interview completely unprepared, wearing ripped jeans and a t-shirt or a polo, stumbling through your answers to the questions and no idea what type of job you're interviewing for, chances are you won't get the job. But, if you prepare yourself and do things to be ready for the interview, your chances of getting it go way up.

The same goes for a relationship, you have to ready for it. You have to prepare yourself for it so that when the time comes and the opportunity to meet your dream partner arises, you will feel more confident in what to do and the chances of things working out will be a lot higher. If you meet your dream man or lady but you're not truly ready for them you may end up doing things that cause your relationship not to work out.

Every relationship is different and each person is different. Depending on what a relationship looks like to you and what expectations you have. The ways of preparing yourself will be most likely be different for everyone

The Seven Ways to Prepare Yourself for an Extraordinary Relationship

Take time to figure yourself out.

The process of figuring out who you are is a huge part of life. Your life. Discovering and knowing who you are establishes your sense of self-worth, confidence, and belief. For some, the process of self-discovery is completely natural, spending time alone helps them to focus on who they are, what their goals are, how they want to live, and who they want to live with.

Think about who you are, not who you want to be. Think about what it is that you need, not what someone else may need. Spend time alone and feel good about it. Time in reflection and self-care goes a long way to building you up.

When Jason Evert said, don't worry about finding your soul mate. Find yourself. Do you try to think over what he meant by that saying? You simply attract what you are.

Be You

The mistakes most people made is hiding who they truly are at the early stage. Hiding for acceptance. It is wrong. When you are putting yourself out there to meet that special someone, be clear and go all out. Don't hide, Don't sugar coat it. Be who you are. Be unapologetically you and seek others who do the same. Be true to who you are and show up as yourself. The one who will love you for you would.

Build and Start Living a Life You Admire

Most singles are always in the habit of waiting for that one person before they are ready to live the life they really adore. For them, they already mapped out the life they want and are just waiting for the right person to push them to start living it. Spend your time on the things that matter most to you. Step into a life that fulfills you, where the only thing missing is partnership. Don't wait for true love to cause your life to flourish. Most often, to attract an amazing partner, you must be an amazing partner. If your life compellingly expresses who you are, you will draw in the perfect person to share it with. It is just the natural order of nature.

Mandy Hale said, Hope for love, pray for love, wish for love, dream for love… but don't put your life on hold waiting for love."

Know What You Are Looking For, And What You Are Not

A person without direction got easily swayed, but one with a direction remain on the path at all cost because he or she has a goal, a destination. This is also necessary in relationship. Define what you want, it's okay to have a bucket list of want and what you don't want when it comes to choosing your partner.

Think about what is most important to you. Pick a few things that absolutely important to you to find in a partner or a few things that are absolutely important not to find in a partner. If you find someone that meets a few integral criteria, you can let go of the rest and compromise on things that aren't as vital.

Remember nobody will meet a hundred percentage of what you want or looking for but as long has the one you meet has a higher percentage of what you want, you can compromise on the rest and even teach him or her the other qualities you look forward to.

Get your affairs in order.

Earlier we said something about been mentally, emotionally, financially ready. It all matter. Spring clean and attend to your finances, mental life, heal from previous heartbreaks, release core wounds, and purge that reservoir of a lifetime's worth of pain that resides within you. Forgive yourself and others for anything and everything they might have done wrong.

Purge toxic friendships, and sort out any unseemly dynamics you have with people in your life. Assess whether there's anything within your power that you would like to change in your life that would serve you and make you more alluring to that special someone

Build on yourself, build on interests, and create a good support system.

There are people who get into relationships and go all in, throwing aside their own interests, friends and even purpose. Having a sense of independence is important even in the strongest of relationships. Make sure you build your life for you, not for finding someone else. It is firstly about you, before it is even about the partner you want to meet. If you build a life for you, that someone else will come and ideally, fit right in.

Do Not Settle For Less or Almost

Everyone deserves to be with someone who love them and you most especially deserve to be with someone who loves you for you. You deserve to be with someone that makes you feel good about yourself, and who you like being with. Don't settle for anything less. If finding your partner means losing you, then it isn't right. Your partner should be the part that complete and complement you awesomely. Life is too short, find that right person, and enjoy it. If you meet someone that doesn‘t feel great to you, move on.

Fill Yourself Up

Remember that ‘perfect’ may not always seem so. You may meet your soul mate and your happily ever after may indeed come, but it probably won’t always be so rosy and happy. That’s okay. Build yourself up in preparation that relationship, marriage and happily ever after aren’t always a bed of rose. No, it certainly isn’t. Roses are beautiful but they also have turns. Your relationship will be smooth as well but not all of the time. You will definitely have your moments. Relationships require a lot of work and attention but if you are looking for the “perfect” relationship that doesn’t include any hardships, you’re going to be looking for quite a long time. Therefore be prepared.

Oprah Winfrey said, “Make yourself a priority. Fill yourself up so that you can give more to others.” When preparing yourself for a relationship, one of the most important things to do before getting into a relationship is to make sure you are completely filled up. Filled up in the sense that you feel like you are already complete without a relationship. If you go into a relationship with the hope that a person will fill a void in your life, that thought and hope of a knight in shining armor coming to save a princess in distress then you are setting yourself up for disappointment.

Often time most people make the mistake of going into a relationship because they feel lonely, if you feel lonely and get into a relationship so that you won't be alone, well let me apprise you with what you may not know. Loneliness and being alone are two different things. These two, people mostly misconstrue, being lonely is a feeling of unhappiness and withdrawal from others while being alone is a physical state.

A good example is of you having the house to yourself, alone but not feeling lonely. Yes, you relate with this, don't you? But you can be married and always have your spouse around, but feel lonely because they don't understand you or spend quality time with you.

Now do you see the difference in both?

Find ways to fill yourself up so that you are so full, you are spilling over with love, gratefulness, happiness, kindness, peace and everything else you want to share. Learn how to give all these things to yourself first so that you are filled up and have no problem sharing with others. It is when you have in abundance of all these things that you consider sharing with others.

The Golden Step

Let's face it, everyone wants to find someone special. We all want to share our magical journeys with someone we love, honor, and respect, as we take a walk towards a beautiful forever after.

How then does this journey start?

Meeting the right person?

Meeting the one who shares the same goes and dream with you?

Dating?

Courtship?

Exactly. Meeting the right person is very important to having a beautiful forever after but is meeting the right person enough?

No, it certainly not. Just as love isn't enough in a relationship, having the right person alone isn't enough either. Of course, with the right person, your journey is made easier, still there are so many thing to do after meeting the right person.

Like what?

Like making your relationship right with the right person. It is one thing to be dating the right person, but it is another thing to be doing it rightly. It isn't news that there are stages before taking the walk down the aisle, and one of those stages you go through before you say I Do to the love of your life is the dating and courtship stages. These two stages serves as the foundation on which you are going to build your next step. Your marriage. If you get these stages right and build a strong foundation, congratulations to you in advance because you have little or nothing to worry about, but if the foundation isn't well laid and you build your relationship on it, oh, but I am sorry in advance.

How Then Can I Build A Strong Foundation In My Relationship With My Partner?

Easy Peasy. Building a strong foundation start with building a strong and good relationship.

What Defines a Good Relationship?

According to Sharp, in a good relationship, both partners feel connected. They respect each other and their differences, enjoy each other's company and feel a sense of security and safety.

Sharp said there's also a good balance between wanting to make your partner happy but knowing that you're not responsible for their feelings. He believes that relationships consist of three things:

each person and the relationship and couples in a good relationship have a strong sense of "we."

Being in a good relationship takes a lot of work and so does starting one, but it's undeniably worthy of it because not only does it steer you in the right direction for a fulfilling relationship, it also helps you get to know yourself and build a strong foundation.

How to Build an Extraordinary Strong and Healthy Relationship

Start Your Relationship with Purpose

You may have come across this phrase, "start as you mean to go on" when it comes to relationships. There are cases of people who were dating just for the fun of it but ended up falling into a committed relationship out of a sense of inertia. These couples may end up living together even when they are unsure if they belong together.

Relationships should be start with a sense of purpose, with the thought about what you want and need, and if the person you are dating is truly likely to align with those wants and needs, as well as yours with theirs.

Communicate

Every relationship is exceptional, and people come together for many diverse reasons. Part of what defines a healthy and strong relationship is sharing a common goal for exactly what you want the relationship to be and where you want it to go and this is something you will only know by talking deeply and honestly with your partner.

Good communication is a fundamental part of a healthy relationship. When you experience a positive emotional connection with your partner, you feel safe and happy. When people stop communicating well, they stop relating well, and times of change or stress can really bring out the disengagement. This may sound simple but as long as you are communicating, you and your partner can typically work through whatever problems you are facing.

Therefore, as with anything, open communication is necessary when it comes to building and maintaining a healthy and strong relationship. In fact, almost as important as having love in a relationship, is couple having and knowing how to communicate especially when both couples are looking towards a long-term relationship, calm, open, and constructive communication is essential when it comes to solving conflict since no interpersonal bond ever comes truly free from conflict but sadly enough, most couple doesn't know how to communicate between each other. Some couples talk things out quietly, while others raise their voices and passionately disagree. The key in a strong relationship, though, is not to be fearful of conflict. Conflict is inescapable in a relationship, but you need to feel safe to express things that bother you without fear of retaliation, and be able to resolve conflict without humiliation, degradation, or insisting on being right. The attitude of a partner humiliating, degrading or just been utterly unreasonable has scared and pushed many couples to shy away from talking and resolving their conflicts. But the thing is, it is in communicating that we find the light to, most of our wants and solutions to our problems.

Unresolved conflicts and the stress associated with conflict put even the most satisfying relationship at risk.

So what is the best way to communicate when it comes to solving conflicts in an intimate relationship?

Definitely burying one's feelings and misgivings, and brushing disagreements quickly under the carpet is unlikely to help. No, it certainly won't help matters. It is essential for couples to first assess the situation in which the conflict has arisen in order to choose how best to address it. When a serious issue is at stake, it is important for both partners to express their opposing views and negotiate the direction of change.

How to Build Strong Communication with Your Spouse

Tell your partner what you need and save them the stress of having to guess

It's not always easy to talk about what you need. For one, many of us don't spend enough time thinking about what's really important to us in a relationship and even if we do know what we need, talking about it can make us feel vulnerable, embarrassed, or even ashamed. But look at it from your partner's perspective. Providing comfort and understanding to someone you love is a pleasure, not a burden.

If you've known each other for a while, you may assume that your partner has a pretty good idea of what you are thinking and what you need. However, your partner is not a mind-reader. No one is actually, and despite the fact that your partner may have some idea, it is much healthier to express your needs directly to avoid any confusion.

Your partner may sense something, but it might not be what you need. What's more, people change, and what you needed and wanted two years ago, for instance, may be very different to what you needed now. So instead of letting resentment, misunderstanding, or anger grow when your partner continually gets it wrong, get in the habit of telling them exactly what you need

Take Clue of Your Partner Nonverbal Clue

So much of our communication is transmitted by what we don't say. Nonverbal cues, which include eye contact, tone of voice, posture, and gestures such as leaning forward, crossing your arms, or touching someone's hand, communicate much more than words.

When you can pick up on your partner's nonverbal cues or "body language," you'll be able to tell how they really feel and be able to respond accordingly. For a relationship to work well, each person has to understand their own and their partner's nonverbal cues. Your partner's responses may be different from yours. For instance, one person might find a hug after a stressful day a loving mode of communication, my husband always, while another might just want to take a walk together or sit and chat and this I is my respite from a long day.

It's also important to make sure that what you say matches your body language. If you say "I'm fine," but you clench your teeth and look away, then your body is clearly signaling you are anything but "fine."

When you experience positive emotional cues from your partner, you feel loved and happy, and when you send positive emotional cues, your partner feels the same. When you stop taking an interest in your own or your partner's emotions, you'll damage the connection between you and your ability to communicate will suffer, especially during stressful times.

Be a Good and Attentive Listener

Talking you may have heard is quite easy, but listening is hard.

While a great deal of emphasis in our society is put on talking, if you can learn to listen in a way that makes another person feel valued and understood, you can build a deeper, stronger connection between you.

There's a big difference between listening in this way and simply hearing. When you actually listen, when you're engaged with what's being said, you will hear the subtle intonations in your partner's voice that tells you how they're really feeling and the emotions they're trying to communicate. Being a good listener doesn't mean you have to agree with your partner or change your mind but it will help you find common grounds that can help you to resolve conflict.

Another thing, most people who maintain healthy, happy relationships, learn to “say sorry and make amends when they acknowledge that they have done something hurtful.

Invest in Trust

Whether it is your partner, friend, or relative, you need to trust them first for there to be any meaningful relationship between you two. A trusting attitude is an attitude for love. To build trust, you need to be consistent with what you say and do. You both have to respect each other’s boundaries. Most importantly, you must never betray their trust. A relationship that has trust has almost everything and often impenetrable by outsider. Therefore to have an extraordinary relationship with your partner, you have to work on investing on trust.

Make Time for Couple Activities

Couple activities help to maintain a meaningful emotional connection with each other. You each make the other feel loved and emotionally fulfilled. There's a difference between being loved and feeling loved. It is when you feel loved, that you get the feeling of acceptance and feel valued by your partner, like someone truly gets you but busy life sometimes get in the way of our spending time with the people we love, even when we live together. The demands of work, for instance, can leave us little time and sometimes little energy to do something enjoyable with our partners. Still you should know that couples who participate in fun activities together also find it easier to stay together, thus allowing the opportunity for building a stronger bond between them. From experience and my research, couples who make time to play games together also had a good quality love life and strong relationship.

Find something that you enjoy doing together, whether it is a shared hobby, reading a book, watching a movie on Netflix , dance class, daily walk, cooking, or sitting over a cup of coffee in the morning.

Try something new together. Doing new things together can be a fun way to connect and keep things interesting. It can be as simple as trying a new restaurant or going on a day trip to a place you've never been before.

Be Playful and Childish

Focus on having fun together. Couples are often more fun and playful in the early stages of a relationship. However, this playful attitude can sometimes be forgotten as life challenges start getting in the way or old resentments start building up. Keeping a sense of humor can actually help you get through tough times, reduce stress and work through issues more easily. Think about playful ways to surprise your partner, like bringing flowers home or unexpectedly booking a table at their favorite restaurant. Put a love letter in his pocket for him to find out at work. Playing with pets or small children can also help you reconnect with your playful side.

Carve Your Own Space

While spending quality time together as a couple is necessary, it is at least as important to spend quality time on our own and allow your partner to do the same. A healthy relationship is a bit like breathing in and then breathing out. Too much closeness can make a relationship feel like a trap and, when taken to an extreme, and a partner gradually isolates their "significant other" from friends, family, and activities that they enjoy, it could be a mark of emotional abuse

Show Attention and Appreciation

While couples are at the beginning of their relationship, the trying to get me to date you phase or after the you have me dating you now phase, the partners often shower each other with affection and words of appreciation. They tend to know what is important to one another and do that often.

But often, as time goes on, partners may start taking each other for granted and forget to show the same kind of admiration they once did. They no longer put the same effort and energy as they did in the beginning of the relationship. There are many ways couple appreciate one another, through gifts, through appreciating their bodies, through words of mouth. No matter how you choose to show your affection, expressing your appreciation of your significant other try to learn and understand what is important to your partner and keep doing at it. And not just on Valentine's, anniversary, or birthday Day.

Be a Team

If there is a problem (you will have tons of those), avoid the temptation of focusing on who was wrong and who should have done and did not do what. Strive to build a strong relationship that solves any and all challenges that come your way. Learn to support your partner when they make mistakes in life; never criticize them when they are at their lowest point. Be their greatest supporter, number one fan. Learn to respect your partner's decisions even when you feel like he or she should have made better decisions. Correct with love and respect. Let them know that you have their best interests at heart. Lastly, a great team is a team where everyone takes responsibility for their actions.

Best Friends

When I was still quite single, I watched a programed it was about the happiest couples on earth, that day, the host brought an old couple to the program as their guest.it was a very interesting show but something stuck. It was the love and respect these old couple still radiates, despite been very old. It was kind of magical. How do the live that long and still much bonded to themselves? I had wondered. But I didn't wondered for long because the host asked y question for me.

You know what they both say? Yes they both answered the question in unison.

"We are best of friends" they had said. And then the husband added, I married my best friend, and every day the bond just got stronger, because she was the only one I would ever want to go to, to talk to, to seek advice from, to seek love, to show my weakness, and blow my trumpet. With your best friend, life is just the sweetest. There is nothing you would rather do without them and doing things together bond you even stronger. And that was why we were still able to be in love up till now and grow stronger in our bonding.

Marry your best friend, if you want to enjoy and have an extraordinary relationship with your partner. Or make your partner your best friend. A best friend knows everything about you, and still stick with you. They know about all the dirty things and still laugh at it with you, making a joke out of everything. I took the couples advice and when I met my husband, I set to make him my best friend, before finally making him my lover. The bond we share, I want to believe is on that has probably never been enjoyed by any couple. But you can share a far stronger one, if you are willing to make or marry your best friend as your partner.

Grow Together

Strive to grow in your individual careers, in your private lives, and as partners, and provide support to one another while at it. Some people, especially wives, sacrifice their careers to take care of their home and babies, only to regret later in life and blame their husbands for it. Avoid that. If your partner feel fulfil working, support her at it, render help at it. You both need to push each other to grow and venture into uncharted territories. Be willing to be uncomfortable in order to grow. If your partner is offered a job in a faraway city and commuting is hard, don't ask them to quit, that would be selfish. Let them go and then figure out how to make your relationship work later on. Don't hold them back.

Understand and Respect Differences

Don't do things in secret because you know your partner won't be supportive of them. An instance was the case of a friend who bought a house behind her husband, the husband later found out and was livid with anger. This single act almost ruined their marriage. The wife thought her husband couldn't be in support, since she was earning much more than her husband. But it became open that the husband didn't have a problem with either, he was actually mad that his wife denied him the support and encouragement deserving of him as her husband.

Secrecy in relationships can be drastic. Instead of hiding, put all your differences on the table and address them one after the other.

Explain to one another why you need to keep doing that which the partner doesn't approve. You don't have to do something with your partner if it makes you unhappy; you only need to understand why they do it, respect that they need to keep doing it, and then give them the space to do it.

Final Thoughts

Be respectful at all times. Emotions, feelings, and beliefs aside, you must always respect the people you love. It doesn't matter if they are right or wrong. You must respect them even if you disagree with them in order to build a healthy and strong relationship.

Respect is food. See it as one. When you feed and hungry dog, it stopped barking at you and start to sway his tail in friendly manner towards you. The same is of the one whom you have shown respect. It will be hard not to win them over. Hard.

Be forgiving

Forgiveness is a key component to a healthy, stronger relationship. Obviously by now, you would already know that nobody is perfect. And no matter how close to complete a soul mate one may find, every individual is still different. And this difference will bring misunderstanding at a point because of our separate mind and point of view. But with forgiveness, couples are able to overcome what may lead to conflict between them.

Partners who practices forgiveness display more behavioral regulation and are more positively inclined towards there partner. These types of couple do not have the time to hold grudges or harbor resentment that can bring anger and bitterness into their relationship. Forgiveness makes you even more connected to your partner as well as it helps you enjoy the presence and saves you from depression and anxiety.

Learn To Compromise

Relationships are built on a give-and-take policy. You have to be ready to sacrifice your resources, emotions, and material things in order to make your partner happy or comfortable. As much as you need to take care of yourself and be happy, you also need to compromise your tastes and preferences if they don't favor your partner. Your partner will sacrifice as well so that you can both find a middle ground.

Be Prepared For Ups And Down

Love just like life is a roller coaster. You must have heard of the saying, life is a roller coaster. I know you want a bed of roses. A sweet relationship filled with love and happiness and at all time, but roses also have thorns.

You have to know that there are ups and downs in every relationship. You won't always be on the same page. Sometimes your partner may be struggling with an issue that stresses them, such as the loss of a job, failing to close a deal, losing a huge contract, not getting a promotion, severe health problems or even worse, death of a close family member. All can affect both partners and make it difficult to relate to each other. You might have different ideas of managing situations like this. Even finances or raising children.

Different people cope with stress differently, and misunderstandings can rapidly turn to frustration and anger.

When time like this arises, don't give up. You need your strength the more, to understand your partner, to love them, and support them. Many partner become a recluse, when going through hard stuff, sending the message they just wanted to be alone. Be persistent in helping them to come out of it. Once you both overcome that time together, your bond would have even wax stronger.

Sex

Sex isn't food, you hear some people say. But it is to some. For most couples, the more sex they have, the happier the relationship and more connected they feel.

Sex is an important part of romantic and healthy relationships. Many people want to have a sexual connection with their partner.

There are many reasons why sex will help you build a relationship.

- It is an opportunity to show your partner love and affection.
- You feel more secure in your relationship if you're having sex often.
- It can simply be pleasurable and fun.
- It help you bond with your partner, and it can be a way of expressing love and care for them.
- It can relieve stress.

Pray Together

Couples who pray together are the most connected to each other. Prayers draw couples together. If you are the praying type, create the time to pray together, and allow God to lead you through in your affairs. Praying together helps you show and receive trust that strengthens the bonds of intimacy in your relationship. It also helps partners to know what the others are struggling with and needs better.

Conclusion

Love you must have heard alone is not enough in a relationship. No it isn't. You need wisdom, knowledge and understanding. This just like love are just part of the ingredient that a relationship needed to survive. They are just like a complementary needs, all are needed to be available for a successful relationship.

Eventually you may have come to realized that what works the most for having an amazing healthy relationship is the effort you are willing to put into it.

It takes a lot of work that is why your determination is about the most important thing in this journey.

A few things to remember

- Always put your partner first. Be compassionate. Love unconditionally
- Learn and practice you partner love languages
- Know the truth; the key to extraordinary relationship is to know your partner's soul and never make them wrong. Understand their needs and do all that you can to satisfy those needs.
- Tell the truth
- Give freedom
- Be passionate and playful
- Be open
- Appreciate and give

I hope you have an extraordinary healthy relationship.

Mitchell Browne

www.ingramcontent.com/pod-product-compliance
Ingram Content Group UK Ltd.
Pitfield, Milton Keynes, MK11 3LW, UK
UKHW022009190726
13853UKWH00004B/1838

9 798533 322201